I0763706

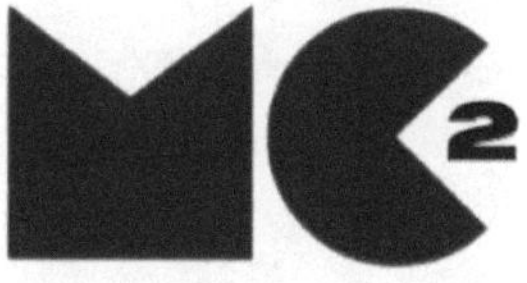

The Barista Thought My Name Was Melancholy

By McCauley

MC² Press

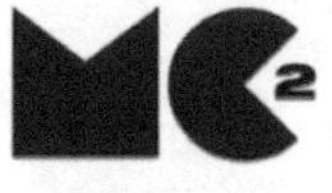

Seattle • 2023

MC² Publishing
A division of MC² Press
Seattle, WA

www.m-c-squared.com

Hardcover ISBN: 979-8-9889153-1-7
Paperback ISBN: 979-8-9889153-0-0
E-Book ISBN: 979-8-9889153-2-4

For, and in memory of,
my mother's father
and my father's father.

CONTENTS

"WE ARE ALL IN THE GUTTER, BUT SOME OF US ARE LOOKING AT THE STARS."

—OSCAR WILDE

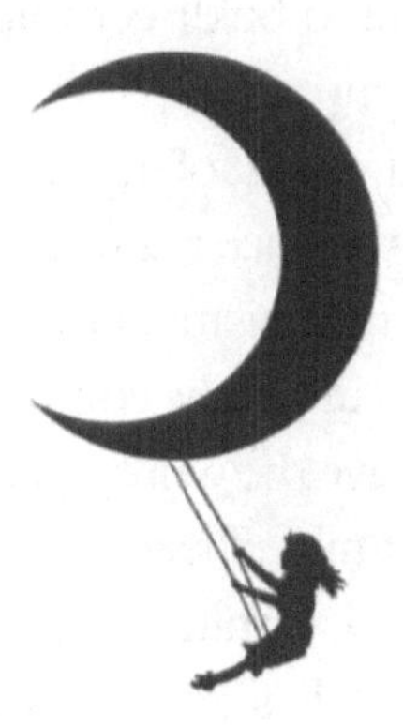

INTRODUCTION

Inspired by a lifelong battle against darkness, *The Barista Thought My Name Was Melancholy* is an ode to the bittersweetness of life. It is my love letter to the lost puzzle pieces that have been hidden between cushions for far too long.

This collection was born from an internal conflict where others' perceptions of me seem to be directly at odds with how I feel on the inside. As I attempted to reconcile the difference, these words poured and poured out of my brain, through my fingers, and onto a screen. I have since realized that both are authentic parts of me—the thick optimism tangled with my voice and the chronic depression I ruthlessly compress. I love the world more than I will ever have the words to express. The irony of it all is that the more I let myself feel the ugliness of life, the more I fall in love with life. Learning to honor the brightest and darkest parts of myself has set my soul free. Further, this dichotomy fuels me to venture beyond my comfort zone. It's not always happy, but it is always exciting. My hope is that sharing these words might help you form a deeper connection to your emotions, too.

Many of these pieces are written from my perspective (as seen through the overuse of 'I' and 'me'). This is not a book about me. *The Barista Thought My Name Was Melancholy* is about the contrast between the brightest and darkest parts of the human experience, using myself as a vessel for its expression. That said, I allowed my imagination to run wild. Every word is based on true thoughts or feelings, but not always my own or reality. In some pieces, I've walked in the shoes of others (real and imagined) but used 'I' or 'me' to allow you to step into those shoes yourself.

I will end on that note. The rest is up to interpretation. **All love.**

SHADOW GHOSTS

For the subliminal heartache that haunts our every move.

THE BARISTA THOUGHT MY NAME WAS MELANCHOLY

There are almost as many ways to say
"I love you"
As there are ways to say
"I see you"
Often, in the same breath—
Infinite permutations of
The only universal language

I think you'd like this song
Here, drink some water
Did you get home safe?
Let's go for a walk
Tucks in your shirt tag
Please, keep the change
Want your usual today...sister?

Rhetorical question; anonymous impression
It's still dark out—nothin' to write about but
The barista knows my order and my corner

There are almost as many ways to say
"I love you"
As there are ways to say
"I see you"

"I have a black coffee for Melancholy"
i.e., I might forget your name but
I love you and I see you

My outfit matches outside
In my corner with my (dis)order
The rest of these pages
Are intended to be permutations
Of both

I love you and I see you
I see you and I love you
I love to see you
I see how to love you

Little else is worth a breath.

UNTEACH ME

Margaritas with the squad
regrets by the pitcher
ended with a dare which
ended with a bridge
that burned when you lit
the gas I poured in
all of the places
you wanted me to.

Once tears extinguished
our fake flames
I refilled my tank
and fueled an overrule
of your rigged game.

But when I left I kept
your lighter in my pocket
because you taught me
all of the magic tricks
but now I am scared
I will burn on accident
so I hide the lighter from me
and I hide me from those
who are still naïve.

Can someone unteach me
how to start a fire?

SCREWDRIVERS ARE LIKE SOBRIETY

The only truth I've known
Is that we all die.

But an old friend found another
One in John Ashbery's words:
Everything is like something else.
Which I have yet to disprove,
Now I see how

Infants are like blank canvases:
        subject to other hands.
Whiskey is like a new log on a dying fire:
        ways to play pretend.
Poems are like pills:
        how they make pain feel like oversized wings.
Screwdrivers are like sobriety:
        needed to do or undo things.
Flowers are like people or snowflakes or days:
        no two the same.
Love is like breath:
        rhythms of giving and taking.
Life is like death:
        unavoidable and uncontrollable.

I now know two truths:
Everything is like something else
And we all die.

COUNTRY ROADS, PLEASE TAKE ME HOME

I wonder about the old farmer
Hidden in the hills of West Virginia
I wonder if he's still hardworking and woodworking
I'd like to get his opinion

Eighty years of caring for those acres
As if he's got eighty more to give
Where did these men go?
How do they live?

I reckon humbly like Mr. Hodgen—
Animals for friends; rapids for music
This land—the canvas of a lifetime
An art that refuses excuses

He let discipline make every decision
So, when the last day is done,
When the rusted gates close for good,
It's his own game that he won

He taught me there is never a reason
To take more than you can eat
There will always be fish in the pond
If you stay deaf to greed

Words that never left his mouth
He speaks one language: action
Silently carving an honest legacy
Immune to all distraction

I wonder about the old farmer
Hidden in the hills of West Virginia
I wonder if he's still hardworking and woodworking
I'd like to get his opinion.

FRATERNAL TWINS

Depression and narcolepsy
Are like fraternal twins
In some ways, they look just the same
In others, not even akin

One of them has been an invisible friend
For as long as I can remember
But only officially
Since last November

They never wanted me to see
How the movies or books end
So they taught me how to
Make all those up in my head

They introduced me to caffeine but
Stole all the energy—I didn't mind
Because they had a Red Bull ready
After every glass of cheap wine

They also give the best apologies
For Irish exits and unanswered texts
Funny, too, "Most Likely to Fall
Asleep Anywhere" their superlative said

Depression and narcolepsy
Are like fraternal twins
Please beware of mistaking the
Former for the latter, like I did.

CRACKED RIBS (19)

March of '19
        began with a Cape Town safari

That week he became a stranger,
        just the boy down the hall
The next week I turned nineteen
        nineteen on the nineteenth of '19
        stupid golden birthday
The next week Bobby died—
        my first funeral speech
The last week my body gave up
        ribs cracked like eggs
        over the edge of the bathtub

March of'19
        ended in the ER.

BORN TIRED

The kind of tired that lives in your eyes
Back there where sink water can't reach
A fire only sunlight can ignite
Optic nerves coated in gasoline

The kind of tired that worries mothers
And they remind you *it's okay to lose*
How do you tell them you'd rather suffer?
You can't, or then they will, too

The kind of tired that cracks bones
After *just one more page*
Midnight—in the zone
Something like the *flow state*

The kind of tired that sleep won't cure
Fatigue never takes a slumber
Waits patiently under pillows to turn
Tomorrow's dreams into thunder

The kind of tired that is contradictory
At least you closed your rings
But watches don't track everything
No way brains don't burn calories

The kind of tired inherited from Father Time
A genetic code for crushing hope
Dreams die in the perpetual meantime
Might as well keep your eyes closed

The kind of tired that coffee can't fix
No matter what the mug says
Different day, same aroma
Smells a lot like indifference

The kind of tired that debuted in home movies
Chew, nap, question, repeat
Then self-expression turns into tantrums
The power of will—an exhausting lesson

The kind of tired that becomes who you are
Solitude is low maintenance until
Fewer conversations yield fewer invites
Yet, tired, still

The kind of tired that is lonely
You are not alone
I feel it too

I'm not sure if this kind of tired is a bug or a feature of the grind. Maybe it is neither; maybe it is both; maybe some of us are just born tired.

You are not alone. I feel it too.

A RIDDLE FOR APRIL

The sun was made on the fourth day,
So maybe a Wednesday or Thursday
Genesis—dawn of the eternal puzzle
This piece: inaudible and intangible
Never misses a beat, always in sync
Somehow floats when we sink
The brighter it is, the darker it gets
One of Mother's many magic tricks
It follows, leads, chases, matches paces
Always, no matter what the case is

Sometimes in front to speed things up
Sometimes behind, but always on time
Left, right, center, depending on the hour

Our dark counterpart in the sun's blaze
Our goosebumps on bright winter days
Our shelter when sunscreen forfeits to rays

A friend and foe, bittersweet company
Shadows are the tax on light's monopoly.

TODAY A MAN FOLLOWED ME

Today a man followed me down 3rd Avenue.
I didn't notice for a while, so maybe 2nd, too.

I'm unfamiliar with the downtown streets.
My ears were covered and filled with Beats.

I relied on my eyes and nose for information.
This man looked and smelled like trepidation.

He circled me twice on his rusted bike.
I really wish I knew my way around Pike.

How ironic—I forgot my pepper spray.
Why me, why here, why today?

I took detours on Marion and Madison.
But I couldn't outrun desperation.

That villain wages war on a whim.
I wish it were safe for me to save him.

DEAR THOSE I'VE LOST TOUCH WITH

Often, grief looks like mourning for loved ones who have lost their lives. This piece is dedicated to those who still have their lives but have lost their place in ours. Grieving for the living is painful, too.

There is value in knowing that you can miss something and not want it back. We are built to grow and adapt, which means that some things get left behind. This is a sad yet hopeful truth. At the end of the day, we are all doing our best, and sometimes finding our best requires distance.

Dear those I've lost touch with,

I love you. I have loved you since our souls crossed paths, and I always will—regardless if this distance is accidental, situational, or intentional.

The memories we share are no less special because we haven't made new ones recently.

You were there for me at a unique point in my life and contributed something that only you could—I can only hope I did the same for you.

I am a different person than I was when our paths crossed, and I'll bet you are too. I'm proud of your growth and grateful to have been a small part of your beautiful journey.

You are irreplaceable to me. Our good times still bring me joy.

I'm sorry for the pain and confusion I might've caused you. We had a special connection. I hope you know that hurting you was not my intent. I am a hurt person myself that tends to retreat. This is not your fault.

Above all, I wish for you to live hard with open arms. I love you.

Sincerely,
Your old friend

CLAUSTROPHOBIA

The doctors told them spring
I reckon I disagreed
Even before I could breathe
I knew winter chose me.

The scar on her belly proves
I stole the right to choose
When, how, where to introduce
What they had produced.

And when I wasn't crying
My eyes were still flooding
So they pierced new tear ducts
For the infant to properly erupt.

THE HARDEST PART

The hardest part was not how it ended,
Or leaving—no, that was easy.
Not the texts we can't unsend,
Or archiving all the memories.

The hardest part was,
Or rather, is
The terror of being that close to someone
Ever again.

HOW DO YOU HUG A GHOST?

Driving down Webbs Road,
A lump jumps in my throat

The old movie begins to play
As I turn onto Burton Lane

There's the character I was cast
Waiting to see me crash

Wish I could cover my eyes
Or give her a place to hide

She lives undiagnosed
How do you hug a ghost?

I'll have to let her be
After all, she's a part of me.

DROWNING IN THE SOUND OF TINY VIOLINS

Everything is so full.
This belly,
This mind,
This heart.
Fuller than deserved.
Heavy, even—
Like really heavy—dense, even.

All this luck taking up space and
Giving buoyancy to the blessings
That float as this big shiny boat
Until the dense, heavy, weight
Of darkness, hiding in the lifeboat,
Cracks the stern floor with relief
And fortune no longer sails.

As it sunk, a doctor in the sky said,
"Even heaven cries sometimes."
So, if medication fills in the cracks
To keep the boat afloat when it rains,
Maybe asking for help is okay.

MAGIC ASHES

There is a sadness with making new friends, knowing
the hue of light we've found will inevitably change
because the glow of innocence fades with age

We start looking for reasons to reach out
instead of dialing with upside-down heads
hanging over the edge of our old beds

Each intermission is a risk that we have strayed
since our last hug, and now we are too far away
to feel the same wonder we discovered that summer

Then the volume of silence fatally
announces that while we were in traffic,
our magic turned to ashes

on the porch where we stood at Camp Bishopswood

atop the lighthouse we kissed and eyelash-wished

running out of luck riding shotgun in your truck

on the field we played soccer and danced all over

buried with every memory at Rock Springs Elementary

on the ring toss handle that taught us how to gamble

in between cobblestones on our drunken walks home

launched off Franklin Street with our late-night dreams

engrained in the canyon clay from that July day

hanging over cliffs like our feet in Europe did

singing the hymns of those quarterdeck bowling pins

all over the fourth-floor study room too, I assume

imprinted into the bus seats that separated our streets

blown out on the cakes from our shared birthdays

in the hammock where we laughed on our secret path

stardust on the roof of that old yellow house is proof

mixed with the volleyball sand by the docks and

the salt in my tears after all of these years.

Perhaps our paths crossed by coincidence
Even so, what a magnificent collision

How lucky I am to know where you're from
How excited I am to watch who you become

What I would do to give you a hug
Maybe this is the price we pay for love.

THE TWENTIETH OF MAY

Yesterday was my grandfather's birthday
The harbor fog was thicker
Trail puddles were deeper
The sky shifted shades of gray

I dreamt of dancing on his feet
When days felt like an eternity
I didn't yet know of mortality
And he lived just down the street

Yesterday was my grandfather's birthday
Would've been 93 on the 20th of May.

THE FUNERAL

Of all the people I expected to see
Your name hid beneath the grief
Of all the people I wanted to see
Your eyes blinded me

Anguish reflected in the stained glass
And I felt it all twice
Once for my favorite dead man
Twice for my favorite dead love.

MONDAYS

Lukewarm water and weak pressure
tell me that it is Monday.

Doors are heavier than usual—
I have to use my sore back to push
and dig my heels in to pull.

The desperation of dehydration
rubs my thumb raw
unscrewing stubborn bottles.

Stairwell steps are taller
than I remember and so
the eroded soles of
my dilapidated boots
slap harder on concrete.

It's winter, too, so my
perpetual cold denies
the luxury of breathing
subconsciously.

And at last,
groceries laugh at me
for not making two trips...
eggs crack on my boots.

To my dismay,
the receipt says today
is Thursday.

Time to hurry up and wait for tomorrow
just like I did yesterday.

THE ZIPPER

Denver Days 2012:
In line for *The Zipper*

Finally tall enough to ride along
With the rest of town, apparently

The only "big kid ride"
The only one with a line

6 PM: in the back by the funnel cakes
I wonder how they make it spin two ways
Cages rotate forward
But the wheel spins backward

6:40 PM: closer, I smell the rusted metal
I like that they don't check seat belts
That takes so long at Carowinds

7 PM: next in line
It smells more like eggs now
The Zipper stops
Attendants whisper, then announce
That was the last ride of the night

A symphony of whines and sighs
Accompany a well-rehearsed vomit routine
I bet it was someone from the East side
We wait
We watch

Unsatisfied until we look the culprit in the eye
How hard is it to not puke?

The cage opens and I learn
My little brother is finally as tall as me

Now I know what empathy means.

WEAPONRY

Even after all this time
My hopes are embarrassingly high
That one day, you will be able to deliver
Just a sentence of the novel left unsaid
Face-to-face in a familiar place,
So we can end the annual midnight text
Though ironically, the timing is now arbitrary
Because it will be on some random day
In a random month, when you finally say

I'm sorry
for using your vulnerability
as weaponry
to turn your nightmares
into reality.

BLACK ROSES

Today I've decided to be lonely. No one asked,
But I want to feel how black roses smell:
Dyed and dying.
Not in a morbid way, no.
In a *carpe diem* way.

How they're dipped in the same dark ink
That flows through my Bic ballpoint pens
When every morning I write on the first
Line of a new page in a Moleskine journal:

Today could be the last.

And how the smeared ink on the
Knuckle of my right pinky finger
Reminds me throughout the day

To live as if it's true.

DÉJÀ VU

Five years ago
Surrounded by glass walls
Code red, code red
The beat drops with bodies
As footsteps harmonize with heart rates
Until these words interrupt the chorus
It was just a drill
I never heard the end of the song
Something like *land of the free, home of the brave?*
Where general education is
Weird versions of hide-and-seek
Lists of names we shouldn't know yet
They sound just like ours
Instead of a glass classroom
Now scrolling through a glass screen
I am reminded of that harmony
On albums of yearbook photos
With new verses of names
Announcing a legacy of infamy
More seconds darkness
Stealing lifetimes of possibility
Negligence is a thief, too
I hear that harmony again

This is a sick game of déjà vu

I hear that harmony again
Negligence is a thief, too
Stealing lifetimes of possibility
More seconds darkness
Announcing a legacy of infamy
With new verses of names
On albums of yearbook photos
I am reminded of that harmony
Now scrolling through a glass screen
Instead of a glass classroom
They sound just like ours
Lists of names we shouldn't know yet
Weird versions of hide-and-seek
Where general education is
Something like *land of the free, home of the brave?*
I never heard the end of the song
It was just a drill
Until these words interrupt the chorus
As footsteps harmonize with heart rates
The beat drops with bodies
Code red, code red
Surrounded by glass walls
Five years later.

WHY I LOVE RED BULL

The rock we chose faces the harbor. To the west, a stew of moorings; to the east, an unforgiving Atlantic. Ahead shines the lighthouse where we watched sunsets—forever our north star.

Dad reads *Ferdinand the Bull*. Brother is now holding Grandpa. And me, I am filming for family. We say a prayer. We hug. We cry. Then we let go of him—Grandpa.

He sprinkles into the sea. The wind carries most of him east and the rest of him onto me.

All I have left of him is the little red book, the old red canoe, and a dash of his ashes stuck in my eyelashes.

And, for all I know, he is floating there still, under his favorite coastal tree, smelling the harbor just quietly. He is very happy.

DEAR DEMONS

For the little voices forever awake in our heads.

NEVER ENOUGH

This is the hardest truth of all
To live in a mind of infinite dreams
Trapped inside a finite being
That inhales a promise:
          "You can do *anything*,"
But exhales the condition:
          "Just not *everything*."

DEPRESSION

I always knew depression was
the battle against sunlight after
sleeping on tear-soaked pillows
next to half-empty glasses because
"hope" was torn out of the dictionary,
confirmed by tantrums over burnt toast
sparking wildfires of self-destruction.

I never knew depression was also
invisible dumbbells on eyelashes,
fatigue that reaches your bones
because nightmares of the past
do not allow slumber past dawn and
solitude becomes a weapon
to fend off their questions.

I never knew
until the diagnosis
but now I do.

NUM NUMS

When I was little,
I called them *num nums*—
the monsters under my bed.

He promised
to scare them away
when he tucked me in.

Between now and then—
I'm not sure when—
the num nums crawled
out from under my bed
and into my head.

"JUXTAPOSITION"

It seems the presence of happiness
Depends on the absence of sadness
And one must know something
To know that it is missing...
Dare I suggest that darkness
Is required for brightness?
If so, why complain?
I would not trade an ounce of pain
I hope you feel the same
And stop pointing fingers to blame
Because if there's truth to any of this,
Might as well give your demons a kiss.

THE BUZZ

A rapper once said that a goddess once said,
"The flowers don't chase the bees."

And I thought,
that is true...but the
flowers still need the bees
if they are to bloom.

So, the bees sting,
and they buzz, but they
pollinate dreams.

So, I guess those
who chase the buzz
will learn, once stung, that
drunk is a dangerous pace.

But I am not one to judge.
I love outer space...
maybe a little too much.

They say addiction is an escape...
sorry, I got lost in the fuzz.

Where was I?
Oh, that's right.

Maybe if we don't chase the
loud ones that try to sting us,
we'll attract the good ones
who pollinate quietly,
and we can bloom silently.

Actually, a wise man once told me
the quietest in the room
are the most powerful,
but I know power doesn't
make it to the tomb.

Down in the ground, nothing
matters much at all.

But if it's up to me, I'd like to rest
where the flowers grow best.

"HYBRID"

Part moon,
revealing different sides,
aligned with the tides.

Part sun,
rising and falling alone,
burning to the bone.

FLASHBACK (I NEED A REFILL)

When you are that little
Feelings should be simple
So you accept the dismissal
That this is all normal

Kids armed with hot glue guns
Naïve to their strength and sting
Burning each other bonded us
Left scars on our innocence, you see

We knew addiction all too well
Tried to run but couldn't from this
Somehow always tripped and fell
The bad blood dried, my point is

The years that end in 'teen'
Were stolen by codependence
Now I won't let myself be
Anything but independent

Twelve was far too young
For identities to tangle
Too young to be undone
Despite it all, I am thankful

If it wasn't real
Why am I still
Trying to heal
I need a refill

BROKEN HALOS

They ask what could be worth
chasing this hard as if the
urgency were explainable...
how do I say I am chasing
nothing and everything?
I am running away
from the tornado in my mind
spinning nightmares of
running out of time.
There is so much to say,
but my voice was stolen again.
These demons live in my head
and no one knows that
I am tired not because
I cannot fall asleep but
because I cannot stay that way.
My invisible roommates,
they shake my pillow
to remind me that
each day could be the last.
I must beat the sun up
to capture every ray
so that I can recycle its light
to share with you and pray
the demons may sleep today.

Maybe they aren't demons after all.
Maybe they are those broken halos
that Stapleton was talking about.

"ANTITHESIS"

each blink
          fights the chlorine
                    as I try to sink
until buoyancy
          reminds me
                    to have mercy

SATURDAZE

It's one of those Saturdays—
I need a triple-shot in my latte
To chase the antidepressants
And the gummy from breakfast

Sipping another latte
In another corner of
Another coffee shop

Manic
    mind
Hollow
    heart
Stoned
    soul

Yet somehow, these lines of rhymes have never been more sober. And trust me, I doubt they're even mediocre. That is fine because I write, without pause, about nine or so an hour.

It is 8 AM
So much Saturday left
So much to hide from
So much to get done

PLAYING WITH FIRE

My
first
memory
lives in my
second year when
I learned how to give
and take peace. Behind bars
of a kiddy gate, impatiently provoking
a rigged game, I demanded the knob of their
door turn, screaming as persistently as time. Scared
by an irreversible conviction that some creature planted
in my mind. It was all trivial (the scariest part). I am sure
because the memory begins with the decision to be stubborn.
To cry and scream with unrelenting fury. I was not hungry or
hurt. For reasons I don't understand, a wildfire lit my insides.
My parents did not answer, they were no match for arbitrary
ferocity. They knew better—attention would fail to put out
the fire. They were right. Only I can extinguish these
flames. Today, the flames are still flying, I am still
alone, consumed by nothing and everything,
but I have more control. The screams
have evolved into words on
this screen that no longer
need extinguishing.

THE SYSTEM

I tried to fight it, and what a fight it was
Armed in loud, flamboyant clothes
Hiding in a sorority house
Rambling to fill silence at any cost
Breathing obligations like oxygen

I was too scared to say that
My favorite color is black
I love thunderstorms
Crying feels more like breathing and
I'm most alive when it's dark out

To love my demons:
This much I have learned
Roommates who give me words to say
Words to help others feel
Everything I don't

But I am no victim
This was all self-inflicted
Suffering is requisite for wisdom
Gratitude is also a symptom
I'm lucky to understand the system

WATER

I hate water.
The more I drink,
the more I cry,
and the more time
I spend in the bathroom
at night.

Please don't tell me to drink more water.
I know that if I want to keep breathing,
I need water, but let me remind myself
that I want air more than I hate water.

I don't hate water.
I'm just tired.

LOW BATTERY 5% REMAINING

I am mostly okay except
For the 5% of me that is
A stranger who likes to sit
On the edge of the abyss
Waiting for a dare to prove
That fear tastes bitter but
The aftertaste is so sweet.

I am mostly okay except
I forgot my charger today.

ANONYMOUS HATE

Naked in a box of one-way mirrors
Every inch of vulnerability on display
Insomnia is a child of this terror
Hidden forever is the only safe place.

"HORIZONTAL"

it has come to my attention
that I am creative only when lying down
the trouble is
my eyes seem to close
before I can create anything
so here I am
writing this stupid rhymeless unpunctuated poem
because I am sitting up

if only I had control
over this shell I'm in

QUESTION MARK ALARM CLOCK

Haven't I paid my debt?
How many tears can a body hold?
Has the flood dried up yet?

When was my soul sold?
Who put it up for sale?
Why is this room so cold?

What are the rules of jail?
Where did my roommates go?
Will they accept words as bail?

Can brains explode?
Do they have meds for creativity?
Asking for the ghost of Van Gogh.

What is it like to be free?
Are my thoughts all I have?
How do I protect them from me?

Why is the abyss so vast?
Could you weaken the exposure?
How long does this flight last?

Where can I find closure?
Whose heart can I touch?
Then, will this all be over?

Can you wake me up?
This nightmare is too much.

NOT VERY ANYTHING

Thank you
for telling me that
I am not very pretty
I am not very smart
and that
I will not go very far.

Thank you again
for gaslighting my tears
because it was all in jest
but it's not so funny when
I didn't ask for a laugh
and especially when
my age ends in 'teen'.

But thank you again
for the gift of independence
for eliminating any chance
I would stay in that town
and that my voice would not be heard
no matter how *not very anything* I am
thank you again.

LONELY LOVE

For the solo journey of learning to live, love, and let go.

THE VOLUME OF LONELINESS

The funny thing about loneliness
is that it amplifies with the
volume of a place.
I've never felt
more lonely
than in a
crowded
space
.

PORCH LIGHT

I'm sorry, I know I'm late
I haven't learned how to operate
With time told by hands
My hours don't look the same

So, I hide from the clocks and
I silence their demands
Notifications on do not disturb
I don't expect you to understand

But I can confirm
I love you despite this curse
Just keep the porch light on,
I'll prove it when I return

Please keep the porch light on
I'll be home before long.

WILDFLOWERS

"Loners," they labeled our box
Under piles of withered lullabies
Blind to our seasonal color
What would've been otherwise

In the next lifetime,
All we ask is this:
Leave us wild;
Let us grow with the wind

One day they will see
That we are wildflowers
Whispering reminders
Things are rarely as they seem.

YOUR DOG

I miss your dog and
how she greeted me
with the gentleness of
a friend you can't remember
not knowing but
might never return

and how
we'd stand together
on the fallen
autumn
leaves
ignoring that   this
would be the   last
fall
in your driveway

other things fell
on top of the
leaves
that next spring
they fell **hard**
they fell   apart

I miss your dog
I wonder if
she misses me
sometimes I miss
the rest of it, too
when *me* was *we*.

FULL MOON

Each full moon, I cry.
Why didn't they tell us
That living is really just
Learning how to die?

WANNABE WRITER

Was it Bukowski who said,
Find what you love and let it kill you?
If so, I found my killer Charles
These words are pouring and pouring
Like Liquid IV racing to save me
From all those nights I forgot.

And was it Frost who said,
Nothing gold can stay?
If so, I am rich, Robert, and I know
My pockets will soon be empty,
But for now, I'll keep breathing
As long as I have a pen and my mind.

So I guess I'll have to live fast
If I wanna be a writer this bad
Before the pen takes my mind.

BLUE BIKE

Nothing seemed so far
As the pedal from my sole
And the moon from my soul
What a shame, who makes
Soulmates that can't touch?
Time is running out. I'm already nine
Neglect leaves a lot of rust
How do I stop the chains from snapping?
How will I get to the moon?
Maybe next year, if I'm given one
God willing, I made it to double digits
Once again, I flex my feet
And the pedal and my toe
They finally meet, but now
I am scared to squeeze the brakes
Moon, why is that?

The fear of slowing down is
One I can't bear, over the summers
I've learned it is much safer
To pedal harder
On the highest gear
Through the cracked hills of
An empty green and the
Music of shoreside gravel
Growls with vibrato
The faster you go
The smoother the ride
I believe the same happens in the sky
But wait...one of the
Blue bikes has broken brakes

Somehow, I hope it is this one

They say I must return at some point
Which means I will have to stop moving
I am scared
What do you do if
You can't reach the ground
Can a sole catch a soul?

I can't hear them anyway
I am flying to the lighthouse
Loneliness taught me how to soar with no hands
So the handlebars become just
Bars
No brakes, no stakes, just a race

Flat wheels bifurcate this forsaken lane
Passing the inn and the wind whistles
Through my ears, "catch me if you can"
The wind is half the reason I am here
The other is thanks to my father
He gives medals for mistakes

I am almost there, but I forgot
The faster you fly
The harder you land and
Blue bikes don't have airbags
Where is my dad?
How do I stop?

My hope was heard
These brakes are broken
I guess I'll have to keep going.

LONG-DISTANCE FRIENDS

Bad timing
        Interest depends
Who's trying
        Pressing send
Comfortably hiding
        Playing pretend
Neither pining
        But never ends
Silver linings
        In our threads
Just surviving
        As long-distance
        friends.

EUPHORIA

No one knows what to do when it rains in California.

If only they'd dance,
they'd learn that screens
aren't the only source of euphoria.

HIGHWAY THERAPY

Listen to the highway on an overcast day...the street signs tell stories of how these scars and stripes came to be—the yellow ones remind you to stay in this lane because your time on this road is not yet over, and if you cross those lines, you are going the exact wrong way until the broken lines wave that you may change your pace; you do not have to wait for anyone, nor do you have to rush through this journey—there will soon be many lanes to choose from and if staying in the middle one is safe for now, there is no need to honk at others who feel differently—they also have things to see, places to be, and we all stop at the same lights eventually, so as long as we check our blind spots and do not live too fast or too slow, we can be whomever we want, sing sad songs, talk to ourselves, scream at the sky, and the highway does not keep score because those scars become landmarks to help others discover that the road will never give up on us—unless we give up on it, so buckle up and keep going.

BAGS OF BURNT-OUT STARS

Woke up looking for a face—
For eyes deeper than the Titanic,
Carrying bags of burnt-out stars.
Coffee breath at twilight speaks
Words picked like Jenga blocks
And the silence that follows is
comfortable. Do such men exist?

BUKOWSKI

This I cannot reconcile:
Inside I feel like Bukowski
But emit the opposite energy
Every inch feels like a mile

Smile, appease, repeat
Words and words to greet
But are they true?
Silence is a liar, too.

IF YOU DON'T

When you find
the longest hour
of the longest day,
remember that no one
is better than you,
and that if you don't do it,
someone else will,
but not as good as you would,
and that would be a shame—
please keep going
we need you.

IRISH GOODBYES

I'm sorry that I have to go
I wish we could share this life
I'm sorry that parties end
I wish I could stay a while

Nothing is left to fix
I'm all out of sunshine
I refuse to tag along
Just to watch flowers die

I know this note won't suffice
Please excuse my Irish goodbye.

SIX-WORD STORIES

Eulogy: read by her third cousin.
History 101: trading lives for land.
Gratuity: ____ I would if I could.
Two-for-one: used wedding bands.

Inspired by Hemingway, of course.

CHAMELEON

everyone knows a different me
blending in with what they want to see
just long enough to lessen
the odds of a question

when you turn your back
I'll quietly fade to black
because the only thing worse than hiding from you
is explaining why I have to

THE MAGIC OF MAINE

I feel most human when all five are alive

When the natural perfume of white pine
Complements the taste of wild blueberries
That are worth every stupid mosquito bite
And fishermen on the water curse for us all
While we watch a ruthless rising tide

God, please keep my senses this alive.

SHOE IN THE SHOE

barely three years
departing the sticky mall slide
only dancing horses in sight
Dad knows the next move
the clock is ticking
who will win: the tantrum or him
he grabs and shoves
left shoe
right shoe
and she's off to the races—
the finish line is the carousel
but she can't run
stops, drops, and cries at once

"shoe in my shoe!!!!"
barely audible
he's confused
he acted in record time
how could he lose

"shoe in my shoe!!!!"
then he sees
the heel of her shoe
was folded inside her shoe

she was, in fact,
paralyzed
by the shoe
in her shoe
I guess patience is a virtue.

CHURCH PLAYGROUNDS

My hippocampus stole most
of those years, but I do
remember the church playgrounds.

We played while Mom was inside,
Dad must've been working.

She had a lot of meetings
at all kinds of churches.

We swung on the swings
and on each other.

But when she hollered for us,
everyone and everything
was always okay.

I'm not sure where
her strength comes from,
I hope I got some.

Now I remember, she said that
sometimes people you love
must go away so that
they can love you better.

Sometimes, for just a little while.
Other times, for a long while.

Just because they go away
doesn't mean you can't play.

SAD POEMS

I write these sad poems
but I promise I'm okay.
There's just so much I feel in my bones,
and can't find the voice to explain.
Because who am I to impose
the velocity of love or the volume of pain?
So, I just write these sad poems...
my words have to go someplace.

THE PLATHEMATICS OF SOULGEBRA

(Sylvia's stories
from Grammy's
bookshelf *[1950s]*

plus

Seattle's stories
from coffee shop
tables *[2020s]*)

times

S^2 *[subliminal
serendipity]*

equals

Shoulders for
new stories to
stand on *[∞]*

*Thank you for sharing,
standing,
solving.*

ANGEL WINKS

For the inexplicable serendipity woven into the human experience.

ANGEL WINKS

I hope

You discover lost sunglasses on your head
The meeting you're late for is postponed
Your connecting flight waits for you
Someone shares extra lunch the day you forget yours
You fall asleep before you send that drunk text
They leave only a warning on your windshield
You wake up on time despite an alarm failure
That you find purpose in the pain

And countless other little things that feel like angel winks
Little reminders that the universe is on your side.

BLUEPRINT

Think kindly
Work quietly
Share audaciously
Grow humbly
Love infinitely

THANKSGIVING JOURNAL ENTRY

I'm grateful for change—in the natural sense—synonymous with growth, transformation, or movement. The only constant in life is that it is inconstant. Impermanence seems to be the only (ironically) dependable aspect of life. I'm grateful for change because of the scarcity it gives to the moment, the challenges it presents, and how it unites us all.

I'm grateful that no matter what happens, the world will never be as it is right now. Knowing that this is all temporary can feel scary, freeing, or both; in any case the impermanence of literally everything makes right now feel like magic. I'm grateful for all the changes that have led to this moment, and for what this moment will contribute to the next.

I'm grateful that existence requires enduring a changing set of circumstances, some of which are uncontrollable. I love that the only way to stumble forward in this journey is to grow because the alternative of complacency is unbearable. Life would be excruciatingly boring without surprises, and the responsibility of adapting to those surprises.

I love the ocean because of its steadfast movement. The waves don't care about anything happening anywhere in the world. No force on Earth is strong enough to stop waves from crashing. The same goes for the power of the sun, the moon, and the circle of life. I'm grateful that these relentless forces connect us all. Knowing that humanity is organized around the same set of natural changes is so unifying. I never really feel alone, despite a tendency to isolate. And for that I am grateful.

WOULD YOU RATHER?

Most footsteps blend with chatter
But her cane adds a different beat
I look to see what's the matter
Tremors must've spilled the coffee

She keeps her wobbly pace, though
I ask her, *didn't that burn?*
With a smile, she says, *very much so*
And I wonder if we share this Earth

We must, because I am also hurt
And I, too, smile sovereignly over my pain
You see, it's a privilege to be burnt
For every scar, I will never complain

This is a right that no one can take
One to wield each day I wake

She mumbles as I leave
Tell me, darling,
Would you rather be
Happy or free?

1789

Finally, an over-the-counter narcotic
Freedom to say everything,
Yet nothing at all

The words that live in your throat
The notes you already wrote
That you wanted to send yesterday
If you could cancel the delivery of pain

The overdue words
The better-left-unsaid words
The wish-you-could-take-back words
And especially,
The silent words
They are all safe here

This is why I cling to poetry
Behind this cryptic facade
I can set my soul free.

P.S.
Anonymity is dangerous for kids
Yes, I can stall for the breathalyzer
But does he still call me stupid?
Sorry I was impatient in the womb
Can we please go back to 1789?
I need to half-write more essays

RED BALLOON

"Where did your
red balloon go today?"

"Up in the sky, it's gonna go to heaven
and one day I'm gonna go up there
so I can go get my red balloon."

"Her red balloon
went up to heaven today."

"Oh, so that's why she's gonna go."

"Yeah, but I told her we didn't
want her to go for a long, long time."

"Because God doesn't want me
to go up there yet."

"Nope, don't want you to go yet."

"That's right, Mommy and I will go
there first and you can join us later."

"Yeah, and where's brother going to go?"

"Don't worry, he'll come too someday."

BRAVE BOY

Brave boy
you do not need to tell me
you are quitting tomorrow
tomorrow never comes.

Bright boy
you do not need big words
to prove an ounce of anything
there has never been a doubt.

Beautiful boy
you do not need to run
from unconditional love
you were born deserving.

All you need
is a mirror and a promise
to love yourself first, you
brave, bright, beautiful boy.

DAYS WITH GRANDPA

Agenda:

A fresh cup of coffee while the sun rises
Stroll to the pro shop to grab the *Portland Herald*
Chocolate chip muffins from the gift shop for breakfast
Pick wild blueberries by the cottage
A harbor-side lunch at the Ledges
Afternoon swim from the Perkins' dock to the rock
Rest, then make dinner with Grammy
A cone of pistachio ice cream from Patty's Sweet Scoops
And watch the sunset at the top of the lighthouse

What I would give for just one more day with Grandpa
He always said *things are never as bad as you think they are*
Look for love in the details and recycle the smiles of others
There's a way out of any situation you're in.

LUCK OR FATE?

Conflating coincidence with destiny
is freeing yet frustrating
because everything becomes both
serious and silly.

HOMECOMING QUEEN

My name sounded funny like usual
Crowned by the crowd for my funeral
Was my mind playing tricks again?
It never matters in the end

I forgot that the price of joy is fear
The spotlight won't let me disappear
I need to hide 'cause I learned early on
Even when I win, I do it wrong

Indeed, even a crown and gown
Were not enough to make you proud
Now I know that all I can control
Is how I feel about myself when I'm alone

So, thank you for the crown
Thank you for letting me down
What a blessing, this lesson at seventeen
Love, your Homecoming Queen.

MY BEST FRIENDS ARE SONGS

Singing "Yellow" at camp gave me wings
When sad, I simply remember "My Favorite Things"

"Free Fallin'" sounds a lot like my heartbeat
Give it up for John Mayer and Tom Petty

Legend's "Nervous" reminds me of every crush
Wallen's "'98 Braves" gives me the same rush

Taylor's first album gave me a "Picture to Burn"
Thanks to *Midnights*, those memories live in an urn

Russ is a red flag for some, but I owe so much to him
Taught me that dedication is louder than any whim

"Tsunami," "Manifest," "Ain't Goin' Back"
Verses that never ever let me slack

Kid Cudi crafted the "Soundtrack 2 My Life"
Plus the "Pursuit of Happiness" knows no strife

Noah Kahan keeps me dreaming about "Maine"
Dreams become reality with G Flip's "I Am Not Afraid"

"The Man by the Coast" and "Preacher" cure grandfather grief
The former describes Grandpa, the latter defines Bobby

Shoutout to the playlist that taught me "How To Love"
And NF's "If You Want Love" for when it's tough

A life better than this one? J. Cole said there's no such thing
Selena nailed it too, had to "Lose You To Love Me"

We didn't know it—but Post was our therapist
I swear "I Fall Apart" is a summary of our messages

"You'd Never Know" by Blu Eyes and "Happy" by NF
Lyrics that helped me take the hardest next step

"Life is a Highway" is for the Carolina coast with Teigs
"Nico's Red Truck" hits different—always on repeat

And "Carolina Can" is an anthem, of course
"Sweet Caroline"—a southern uniting force

Gun to my head, I'd say that country is the best
That I only realized when I moved out West

And we have to throw "Sirius" in there, channel 23
These songs, my best friends, set my soul free.

CONCRETE DOG PRINTS

Imprints no one would forget
He stormed right through
The concrete was still wet
I wonder if the dog knew

I'd like to think so
That's what I tell myself
When it's time to say no
For the sake of something else

But we are all fools
And this game is rigged
If you're gonna break the rules
Might as well break 'em big.

LETTER TO SANTA

For schools to be safe
For cynics to sing a new chorus
For unity in the human race
That's all I want for Christmas

The symphony of footsteps on stairs
The smell of secret family recipes
The answers to prayers
Instead of coal for enemies

A castle for the dreamer
A hug for the grieving
A lover for the loner
Wrapping paper for feelings

For friendships to reconcile
For politics to melt away
For cheeks to hurt from smiles
My wish, for just one day

The brand-new pajamas
The competition for cookies
The beautiful chaotic drama
For family tradition rookies

A chance to right my wrongs
A blank canvas for next year
A new playlist of sonder songs
More love and less fear.

PRITCHARD

I spy dice in the air from the window above the stairs
Two minutes on the microwave; we open a new case
Drunk and hungry, but never angry.

Because even when He's Not Here, I know
They live behind Larry's—right by Noble Street so
I have someplace to go when no one can walk me home.

Again, on the roof, counting double stars
Laughing til we fear we're all out of beer
This is when the photo-taking begins
My favorite goofs, albums filled with them.

April 4th is the date and blue jerseys float with grace
Playing on a sea of wrinkled white bedsheets
Until a tsunami of pride drowns our halftime dreams
It's too bad seniors won't hear, "Maybe next year."

Although no flood can wash away this love,
It's time to turn tassels, goodbye, our yellow castle.

COULDN'T EVER FIGURE HIM OUT

My father—quite the character
Grew up a wrestler
Hated saying *yes sir*
Helped save dolphins
Then went broke as a builder
Tiny home in Nicaragua
But his soul lives in Maine
Where he was a camp cook
And taught kids how to canoe upstream
Mixes butter in his coffee
Helps with ketosis, apparently
Taught himself guitar and ukulele
Taught himself everything, actually
Proud graduate of YouTube Academy
You'll probably find him in cowboy boots
He's from Jersey, though
Don't let him fool you
An outdoorsman by trade
A technologist by hobby
But an artist at heart
Sings that he's free-falling
But he figured out the building thing
One of the best in town now
His eulogy will read:
"We couldn't ever figure him out"
But his legacy will be:
"If you don't care what they think,
You can be whatever you want to be
And if you work hard enough
You'll be a damn good one."

RAIN IN CALIFORNIA

Some satirical curse—
The legend of rain in California
Pulling crocodile tears of thirst
From innocent flora and fauna

It always begins slowly
Then pours all at once
An answer from the Holy
After unrelenting months

She rarely drinks water
(It rarely rains in California)
Tsunamis finally taught her
Thirst carries trauma

So, let's water the flowers
With a slow, steady stream
So that when it showers
Roots protect her dreams.

HYGGE

"What is your favorite word?" An angel asked us
He replied like he'd been waiting for the question
"Hygge," a feeling of warmth and coziness
I wasn't so quick, but there's only one it would ever be
"Godspeed," a wish for success on a risky journey
The angel winked and while we kept working
They must've written something on the walls
To keep the boy east while I moved west
We only shared that room for a short while
Just long enough to make leaving bittersweet
What a shame we don't want the same things.

DEAR FUTURE

Dear Future,

Please do not flatten our hills
Have patience for our accidents
We could use some calluses
Instead of all these pills.

Sincerely,
Gen Z

GROCERY SHOPPING

I cried in the grocery store parking lot today
Some guy couldn't be bothered to put his cart away
He looked to see who was watching but missed my gaze
He left it in the rain, taking up a whole space
Then an older man in uniform had to run a long way
Just to catch the cart as it rolled further and further away
He slipped with my faith but bounced up with grace
And the first guy, well, he drove right past and waved
My hope fell as tears, how sad is the human race
Worst of all is that I am the same; I need to pray
I'm sorry for every day I have left things in your way
God, please craft a just and gentle fate
I promise to always put the grocery cart away.

MY HOPE

I find hope in:

The way strangers who are shy
whisper that your shoe is untied.

When we look back to hold doors
for others when rain pours.

How we can't help but say *bless you*
after a sneeze across the room.

When they act blind to puffy eyes
so you don't have to explain the cries.

Chain reactions of buying coffee
for whomever the next in line might be.

That we love by default,
often to a fault.

At the end of the day,
we are gonna be okay.

GROWING WINGS

For choosing to find light in the darkness.

TINY SUPERHEROES

I heard there's a child
That no one can see
Who longs to stay wild
Dreams of who they will be

"Superhero is no occupation"
So they settle for a degree
Now used as a decoration
To hide what else could be

But this happiness equation
Is optimized for conformity
It cancels out imagination
To solve for authority

You hear the child, too
Beating in your chest
I'm here to tell you
It's okay to fail the test.

THE BOY ON WEBBS ROAD

Yelling and strumming beside Webbs Road
While he waits for our bus to show
Brings that old guitar everywhere, somehow
In this *everyone knows everyone* town

An epidemic of street signs and stoplights
Inevitably spread over county lines
I no longer hear the boy or his guitar since
Taking Blades Trail makes more sense

The street signs are stolen anyway
Truck beds make sorry hiding spots
Another lesson learned the hard way
Try the shadows at the boat launch

Friday night lights drown most of us out
Shining on stars of rival county schools
Win or lose, we'll take 16 to Cookout
And laugh for hours in hierarchal booths

Still got half a tank for backroads
Courts or docks? Submit your votes
Let's pretend these nights will never end
At least until the H.O.A. gets wind

Some of us are still playing pretend
Others of us are trying to forget
Unless you're the boy on Webbs Road
I'm sure he's cracked the code.

MARCH 8TH

In 1869, Susan and Elizabeth were visionaries
Daring to add "suffrage" to the female dictionary

In 1908, more and more joined their fight
15,000 women marching for a stolen right

In 1909, International Women's Day was born
No suffrage in sight, but a win, to be sure

In 1911, one million rallied for the dream of equality
And the Triangle Fire stole 146 souls, tragically

In 1913, the world decided on March 8th to honor
The strength of women, and those lost in blue-collar

In 1920, congress conceded the 42-year-old amendment
The 19th: a prime number, indivisible, and independent

In 1963, Kennedy's signature assured equivalence
But it seems we are still making up the difference

In 1972, Nixon followed suit with Title IX at last
Great-grandmother dreamt of the day they'd pass

In 2023, we've gotten good at raising voices
Let's not forget the privilege of speaking through choices

In every breath I take, every morning I wake
I am proud to be a woman, especially on March 8th.

ME VS. ME

On mornings when indifference is all I can feel
This internal dialogue gets me out of bed:
Responding to my own "you won't" with "I must"
Who I was yesterday is my biggest competition
Making every day a new game of me vs. me.

EYES

closed eyes
the perfect guise
to hide from skies
and still, find highs
until the soul replies
it is time to realize
the duty to analyze
how this all applies
to a game of improvise
and reach compromise
that will not surprise
well-intentioned allies
or provoke the spies
to kill the wise
because the sun will rise
no matter who dies
so, focus on the ties
not the goodbyes
love is life's prize
open your eyes

BUT I LOVE MY NAME

I haven't yet figured out
the urge to have my words heard,
but the ache to be invisible.
I could use a different name,
but I love my name.

BE LIKE MIKE

I still wanna be like Mike
knowing when to strike
making up a story
marking champ territory
leaning on commitment
believing when they didn't.

Greatness is a decision
of calculated precision
required every minute
especially at your limit
that's where legends live
there's always more to give.

STOP

Using their definitions to
Answer their questions in
Their old schools just
To follow their silly rules.

Congratulations
You've grown wings
A lonely celebration
Flying high above kings.

But you are free now
Even if no one can see
Take your floating bow and vow
To be yourself, forever free.

FIREBALL

Beware
of loud voices
shouting that
the world is round.

I believe it,
but not because
they shout it.

I believe it
because when I find
the highest places
to watch the fireball rise,
its flames illuminate
the slightest of curves
in my periphery,
and that is why
the world is round
to me.

But why would I
believe the shouters?
Why would anyone?
My eyes are different from theirs.
I must see this world
for myself.

And the more I see,
the more I need
to close my eyes.

Until dawn, when I am reminded
of all those words they shout,
the ones my eyes don't see,
the ones my hands don't meet,
and I relearn that no one,
anywhere, ever,
really knows
anything
at all.

DAILY PRAYER

Hello and thank you for this day
Respectfully, I'd like to say

Please humble me relentlessly
I am ready to serve maximally

Keep me where my feet are
Grounded, no matter how far

Make me pay for my impatience
As I grow more and more audacious

I promise to learn from your love
And to greet enemies with hugs

Thank you for this day again
I'll say the same tomorrow, *Amen.*

KINDNESS

Kindness cannot be taught, only learned
Kindness is not a synonym for charity
Kindness is not interested in optics
Kindness is not fleeting nor discretionary
Kindness is not claimable—least of all by me
Kindness cannot be reduced to a noun
And kindness is not ever regrettable

Kindness is joining the person eating alone
Kindness is knowing when to walk away
Kindness is sharing songs, books, or words
Kindness requires vulnerability
Kindness is bringing extra just in case
Kindness is a default setting—a way of being
And kindness gives more than it takes

Kindness always wins.

WINGS

I've always preferred candles to bouquets
I'd rather watch flames fly than daisies die—
Glowing proof that oxygen brings wings
So that I can soar above any war until
It is my turn to float with the smoke
Up high where flowers don't die.

DEEP BREATH

Today feels like
a deep breath when
you have a cold.

Hours pass slower,
music sounds softer,
and it hurts a little.

But soup tastes better,
I sleep longer, and
it could hurt worse.

Today feels like
a deep breath, and
I'm learning to exhale.

ODE TO OLD FRIENDS

Old friend
I am so sorry
We didn't break, just bent
I will never forget

Holding our breath on bleachers
Fireworks on the lake
Sharing favorite teachers
Giving shoulders for heartbreak

Studying for hard tests
Brutal soccer games
The prom night mess
All of those French braids

Friday night tailgates
Adjacent parking spots
Styrofoam Cookout plates
Meet you at the boat launch

My Brother's Bagels
The goodbye left unsaid
Ambiguous labels
Let's drive backroads instead

Now I can't tell you
I will never forget you
I hope this poem will suffice
I'll love you for the rest of my life.

THANK YOU

Thank you for doubting
Thank you for leaving
For waking my dreaming.

I did not freeze into stone
I spun your cruel into fuel
I can do this all on my own.

HOW YOU DO ANYTHING

A football coach told an old friend who told me,
"How you do anything is how you do everything."
I believe it's true, which haunts my every move

Ever since that day, I haven't been able to do
Anything halfway, which is a blessing and a curse
Because the pressure is worse, but so worth it, too

Anything I do is now bulletproof, so to that coach,
Thank you for this approach...it slows me down,
But I spend less time on the ground because

It's hard to do anything great at that rate,
And *how you do anything is how you do everything*,
So, it's a good thing I made my bed this morning.

CURRENCY OF LIFE

Fearlessness is glorified
We are all born scared
Every day I wake up terrified
Knowing my soul is impaired

Eventually pain becomes purpose
Fueled by the power of will
Convince yourself it's worth it
Then the mountain becomes a hill

Maybe imposter syndrome
Is a feature, not a bug of the grind
Testing who you'll become
When fate and courage are aligned

Sure, risks are scary
But regret is a heavy weight to carry
It turns out the grind has a price
The currency of life is sacrifice.

BOTH

My wish is that you learn that it is not wrong to laugh while you cry. There are no laws against smiling during arguments or hugging an enemy. You can be both—stoic and goofy, smart and silly, depressed and optimistic.

This is a collection of poetry and prose
To remind you that we would not know highs without lows
What a blessing it is to feel both.

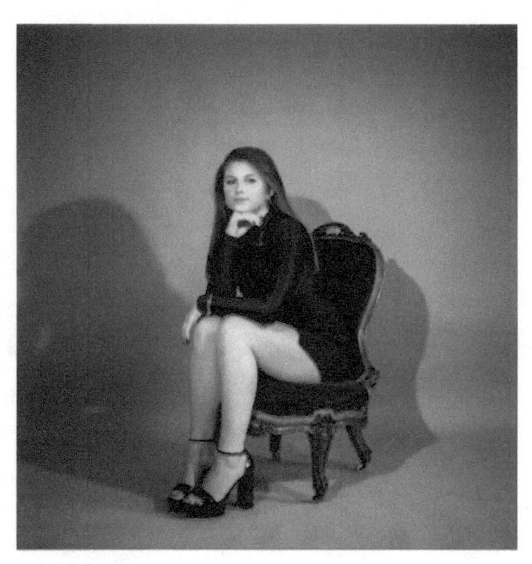

ABOUT THE AUTHOR

Raised in a laissez-faire household in a small North Carolina town, as a little kid McCauley packed her own lunch, did her own laundry, and was often the only girl in her karate classes and t-ball teams. Her father stressed independence; her mother demanded kindness. The only other rule was to make your own.

All four of her grandparents were alive, married, and living within 45 minutes of her childhood home until she was 19, which she considers to be the greatest blessing of her life. Much of her work is inspired by the stories and wisdom they shared, along with mental health and addiction patterns she's observed. She now lives in Seattle, where she peacefully blends into a sea of introverts, spending most of her time writing in coffee shops.

www.ingramcontent.com/pod-product-compliance
Lightning Source LLC
LaVergne TN
LVHW090526110826
845146LV00003B/992
* 9 7 9 8 9 8 8 9 1 5 3 0 0 *